THE ULTIMATE LANDSCAPE GARDENING FOR BEGINNERS GUIDE

DESIGN YOUR LANDSCAPE TO TRANSFORM YOUR GARDEN

and are the owned by the owners themselves, not affiliated with this document.

Table of Contents

Introduction

Chapter 1:What is Landscape?

Chapter 2:What is Landscape Gardening

Chapter 3:Landscaping Tips

Chapter 4:What Tools Should Not Be Missing For The Care Of My Garden

Chapter 5:Preparing the Soil for Planting

Chapter 6:Rock Garden for Landscaping

Chapter 7:Using Plants for Colors and Textures

Chapter 8:Garden Landscape Ideas

Chapter 9:Climate for Landscape

Chapter 10:   Landscaping with Trees

Chapter 11:   Edible Landscape Gardening

Chapter 12:   Berries and Weeds for My Edible Landscape

Chapter 13:   Tips and Tricks for Growing Healthy Herbs and Vegetables

Chapter 14:   How to Defend Against Plant Parasites

Conclusion

Introduction

When you plant and care for a garden you experience something that is truly gratifying and fulfilling. As you watch flowers bloom, herbs grow, and both fruits and vegetables ripen you are satisfied with and proud of your accomplishments. Not only are the flowers beautiful and calming, but you are able to use the produce and herbs you grow to make more delicious meals, sustain your family, save money, and benefit the environment. By gardening you get to experience something that along with being helpful and fulfilling is also peaceful and fun.

By choosing organic and natural options to garden with, rather than the synthetic chemical-based fungicides, herbicides, pesticides, and fertilizers, you can benefit the earth and environment. It may seem like a small change, but as people continue to make the change to organic the beneficial effects will grow and the earth will gradually heal from the chemicals, we have poisoned it with. By choosing organic gardening you can naturally fertilize the earth with options that will refuel it with the minerals and vitamins it requires in order to grow healthy plants that will nourish those who eat them.

It doesn't matter if you have a green thumb and years of experience with gardening or if you are a complete beginner. Maybe you tried to grow some plants in the past and they always died, that's okay! With the right approach and knowledge, anyone can grow a successful garden yielding fruits, vegetables, herbs, and flowers. All you need are the right tools of knowledge, which are provided within these pages. Let's explore some of the basics of the organic method to get you on your way to success!

Before you focus on the ever-important soil, watering, and planting of your garden you first must plan. When gardening, it is important to know the size of your garden, the hours of sun access, wind, and more. All of these factors will greatly affect what you can plant and how well your crops grow. Thankfully, with a little knowledge, you can plan the perfect garden.

If you live in an apartment then you really only have one option for a garden, which is to practice container gardening. Thankfully, there are many options for container gardening and you would be surprised by the crop size you can yield.

If you live in the suburbs or city with an average-sized yard then you should find that your garden is easily accessible from your house. Even if your backyard is on the smaller side, you should be able to plant a decently large garden if you practice gardening by the foot. With this gardening method, you can maximize your gardening space and crop yield with a little extra planning.

If you live on a large property you can have an especially large garden. You will likely be able to not only provide enough crop yield for your family, but even excess to sell at the local farmers' market or to gift to neighbors if you desire. However, if you do live on a larger property try not to place the garden too far away from your home or a place where you regularly walk past. You want to be able to easily view and examine the garden on a daily basis so that you know when it needs to be watered, weeded, or harvested.

Chapter 1:   What is Landscape?

By nature, for a building is to be correctly defined as "landscaping" (verb form), on the grounds of the property, you have to make modifications (or maintain past changes)-in either a realistic or imaginative manner. In an extended sense, everything that happens outside the house on the premises is part of the landscaping of a home itself. A similar term is the "landscape." You're engaging in landscaping while you're landscaping your yard.

Simply placed, if you may look out your window and see a particular feature in your yard that affects the overall aesthetics or usefulness of your house, then that feature is part of the "landscaping" of the house. It should also be noted that even though they remain overlooked, some of the technical aspects of one's landscaping, such as underwater drainage networks, are significant.

Stay in Harmony: Landscape and Estate

While the above provides a basic, practical definition of the term "landscaping," first-time homeowners are far more likely to profit from a rundown of the sort of work they may do (or hire a contractor to do so) to upgrade their yards.

There is a significant issue to think about before we continue. Will one house be harmonious with each other, and its landscaping? We're not talking of practical things like rising shade trees to the south of your house in order to reduce the cost of energy. Would the way your house looks affect landscaping choices, such as plant selection and design, or whether a wooden deck or concrete patio will be constructed?

A number of homeowners prefer to plan their houses and landscaping colorfully. That's relatively straightforward, but how far are you going to harmonize the house and yard in an esthetic way? For example, if your home type does not classify it as a "cottage," can you still landscape the theme of a cottage-garden? Yeah, but you can only determine the degree to which you can aspire for this kind of happiness because the flavor of all is special. There's no question that certain styles of hardscape elements match some houses better than others. For, e.g., a rustic-style roof looks much better applied to a log cabin compared to a contemporary ultramodern one.

Intuitively this is also possible to achieve equilibrium. And if you decide to match your house with your landscaping more seriously, you may have to take it to the next level: landscape architecture, which is basically a theory of art (although this discipline rarely loses sight of realistic concerns).

Note, prospective customers can't convey their private desires — that's what you, as the seller, need all this work. First of all, you don't like outdoor puttering; you do not need water features in your house, so the color doesn't matter in winter. And still, homebuyers checked the pattern. Following are the common things regarding landscaping that you can do:

- Residential environments under-maintenance. To begin with, if there is a choice between a trees' dwarf version and a larger version, select the dwarf tree — it won't need to be pruned as much.

- They build waterfalls, fountains, and ponds. The most impressive projects require concentration or focal point. A well-done water element is a focal point that can create a difference between the property and the other properties.

- Visual attraction year-round. Evergreens and lots of berry-growing shrubs are ideal antidotes to the bleakness of winter.

Below are only a few suggestions for the home landscape to motivate:

See what a lot of people do with their home design designs. If appropriate, speak to them about the reasons behind their choice for home landscaping products, and their feelings.

Newspapers, magazines, television, and the internet do provide a wealth of information regarding what "online" types of home landscape designs really are.

Ask specialist consult for the area of landscape architecture

If you don't want to pay for guidance to a landscape planner, try some tips from your nearest nursery, at least.

Real estate agents track day in and day out the responses of prospective customers to home landscaping; inform them on developments.

How to Landscape?

When it comes to determining whether to plan your outdoor garden, there are just a few simple rules to remember. The fundamental idea that matches the purpose of the form is at the root of those concepts. The form and style of the space determine how you want it to be used. First, you'll study these easy-to-follow ideas before you start "how to landscape," and then you'll be on the road to a beautiful landscape being created.

What are you doing, and what do you want? Are you waiting for a playground, a quiet place to read, or a mix of the two? You might want a spot in which to grow your favorite cooking herbs and vegetables. Make a list of your expectations and create a rough picture of how this situation is to be overcome. Following are the ideas that you have to keep in your mind in order to landscape: Benchmark the Yard

Firstly, assess your yard. Which is The Way of the Sun? Build seating areas with shrubs and trees that are out of step with prevailing winds, or block and wind lead. Locate the sunniest areas, and identify the right places to plant. Ideal for finding a place to rest and enjoy, shielded from the daytime heat. It is also wonderful to build a room on cooler days and to take advantage of the sun's warmth. So, consider how you'd take water from one part of your yard to another. Start with sun angle measurements and establish a watering technique to know how and when to plant.

Exist in It

Staying in a bed is nice until we move in. Unless you sit in one place and spend time in one room or another, you don't realize whether or how that works in with your strategy. Turn back a chair to pick a fresh place to get up for the day. Notice potential focal points, and how they relate to your views of home and glass. How do known routes already function inside the mix? Paths that interact with the world impact the users' interactions, not just to direct them from one location to another, but to involve them as well.

Keep It Simple

Generally, the simplest answer is the best. No need to make the final decision more complicated or more extensive. Then, they have just the items that concern most. Start tiny and continue with a structure allowing you to easily switch to a flower bed, veggie plot, or patio from the inside of your home. Intuitive is still the right solution to the issue. If you overlook an actual walkway, for example, the direction, you built up through the lawn may be a guide to the most convincing layout.

Loaned Opinions & key Points

Outside your yard, do not hesitate to take a drink in the view. Strategic positioning of trees to encircle existing views. Incorporating a tree as a focal point or a collection of trees to build new views. Sheltered plant trees offer bright colors in the autumn, in the summer. Find the flowering trees like dogwoods, buckeyes, crabapples, etc. Crop gardens, as well as perimeter forests, establish colorful focal points. To complement and enliven your outdoor experience, grow a collection of hydrangea-like flowering shrubs along with a patio or porch.

How Do You Want Your Plants?

A garden without plants is not a garden. Hold the plants you wish to expand on the running list. Then circle back to your site assessment to see what's possible. That will keep you in some shade from plants enjoying the sunlight. Assure that a watering plan is drawn up based on plant needs. Determine that equipment suits the construct well as having a heavy-duty hose with a watering thumb control nozzle and a timer.

Embrace Alteration

There's one thing that is discovered during years of rising and planting, it's that nothing remains the same. You can select a new route, or your patio is too narrow. And so, your countryside is evolving and changing.

Chapter 2: What is Landscape Gardening

Landscape gardening is one of the best choices available to turn your garden into a place of dreams. Many people earlier assumed that only the interiors required attention, as it is the interiors alone that add to a home's look. However, growing numbers of people are now opting for landscape design ideas to offer a fresh and attractive look to their home and garden.

With a variety of landscape magazines offering excellent ideas for landscape design, there's really no dearth for ideas. The internet is yet another information storehouse, as it offers fresh and fascinating ideas along with pictures showing the plan's final outcome. You will get an idea of what designs various people are using to beautify their gardens. Landscaping is an inexpensive concept, given that you know how to do it.

Planning is the first step to a successful project in landscaping. You will know exactly what you want and put on paper specifics so you can work your way to complete your whole plan slowly. Having advice from a professional landscape architect will help you eliminate from your design all the trouble areas and make sure you have a beautiful landscape plan. The landscape architect will be able to include some beautiful and realistic, fresh ideas.

A landscape design must be such that the usage of available resources is maximized. The natural elements are also a great influence on any given area, so the amount of sunlight, water, wind, and terrain are all important factors that need to be taken into account in order to create a good landscape design. What you need to consider, though, is that another person's landscape design does not fit as it is for you. It is important that you get good ideas for the landscape and then customize them to suit your needs.

Plants, trees, and flowers have always been a common landscaping feature that almost instantly makes the garden look beautiful and is also simple on the wallet. Plants that are suitable for the different climatic conditions should be carefully selected. It is best to look for plants that do not need a great deal of maintenance time and energy. Water fountains and other bodies of water are another lovely and eco-friendly concept of the landscape. A healthy green lawn is another feature you might add to your garden to make it look lovely and beautiful.

The budget is a significant factor to bear in mind when you start on your landscaping project. It's important to do a good survey so you can find good, cheap material to make your plan a reality. One idea of landscaping is a walkway that adds charm to your garden and, at the same time, makes your evening walk in the middle of nature easier. It is a good idea to use rocks, bricks, and other stones to make it look natural and elegant. Advice from a certified professional landscape architect will help instill fresh and interesting ideas for landscaping into your design.

Chapter 3: Landscaping Tips

First, design your landscape on paper. Begin by listing the functions your landscape should provide your family, such as play areas for small children, entertainment areas, and shade. Next, decide where these functional areas should be located for maximum pleasure and use. Consider wind patterns, sunlight, accessibility, and other site-specific conditions when creating your landscape plan.

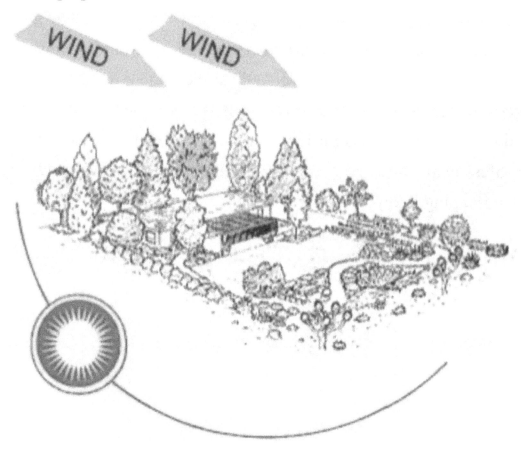

Here are some useful facts to consider when designing your landscape:

- When selecting plants, consider function first and foremost. Next, decide on acceptable maintenance levels. Group plants according to irrigation needs whenever possible.

- Always select plants according to how their mature size and appearance fit into your design. Do not select plants based on initial appearance in immature stage of growth.

- Consider adding interest and color to your landscape by rotating annual flowers in small "investment zones" near your house.

- Plants that are placed by themselves and directly exposed to the sky.

- Large growing trees should be planted at least 20 feet from your house. This gives tree roots adequate space to grow and prevents structural damage to your home.

Paths in a carefully designed sequence, or applied on a larger scale to the movement of people in cars, such as the design of motorway planting for viewing at high speeds.

Unlike architecture, landscape design is concerned with living material, which not only grows changes during the season & over time, but also moves in response to wind or to the touch. Thus, the kinetic experience is enriched and made more intimate and varied. The positioning of groups of planting relatives to the path can influence the movement of the observer.

Where a change of direction is desired, ground covers as well as tree & accent shrubs can be used to create pivots point at which one is physically and visually forced to change direction. Pivot points can be extended to form bridging points across paths & roads. If the bridging points are sited close together, these in turn create tension points in the design where the space is narrowed down or constricted before opening up & expanding into another space. Using the idea of line of line of movement, the design can be given a momentum of its own which can be described as a "design speed'. This can be static, slow, and moderate or fast; the inherent design force built into any line movement is self-expressive.

Certain misconception exists relating to design line movement. All too often designers seek to create line movement by giving a wavy outline to planting beds. Tree & shrub planting will itself create all the wavy line movement at a higher level as it grows.

Plant material junction should not be too acute. Where the design line movement abuts a building, or two paved areas meets grass areas, the acute point formed results in an awkward space for planting & should be avoided where possible.

Access, Vistas and Arrangement: The point of entry into any given space is always of crucial importance in the design. For instance, one may choose to make it discreet or emphasize it by enfacement. A drive or access road into a site may have predominantly vista -like qualities, which can be reinforced with banks of tall & medium shrub & ground cover. Planting flanking each side. The long-accepted tradition that when one entered a site, part of the building was first seen & then lost from view, to reemerge later, still remains an effective design technique.

The principle of enfacement can be used effectively to draw attention to specifically desirable views & possibly to block out the less desirable elements. For instance, massed foreground planting may be used to screen the near view, larger framing plants placing the emphasis on the distant view. Enfacement of certain views in connection with doorways or atrium courtyards can best be achieved by the use of large vertical shrubs or small trees with a horizontal branches structure.

Anchoring as a design technique is akin to enfacement in so far as it has a similar design purpose that is to control corners & portion of the design which need reinforcement. The planting of dome-shaped shrubs at the base of small sculptural tree or shrub is another form of anchoring.

Landscape Design Guidelines

The walls, ceiling and floor are the dimensions of the outdoor "room". A ceiling (the sky) and a floor (the ground) are always present, though they might require modifications. The walls are created as part of the landscape design.

The structure of anyone of the three dimensions mentioned above may affect the appearance of the other two as well as their functions.

The landscape's walls are responsible for screening, wind protection, framing of off property views, enclosure, and so forth.

The ceiling of the landscape provide shade, protection from weather elements, passive solar heating, and so forth.

Structural walls for the landscape include many types of walls and fences. They offer the advantages of full height from the start, limited groundcoverage, and variety of materials.

The most satisfactory landscape walls often combine both structural and planting materials.

The principle concerned with ceiling structure in the landscape is for shading purpose. Shade may be provided by structural roods, awning, arbors, or the like or by shade and ornamental trees.

Good shading units depends on accurate recognition of the time of day when the shade is necessary, the path of the sun over a property, and the angle at which the sun penetrates the area during the time shade is needed. Further recognition of the density of shade desired is also necessary.

Tree placement must be based, in part on above and below ground utility structures that might be affected by -or affect -the tree's branches or roots.

The light and shadow patterns created by the landscape's ceiling structure are extremely importantly aesthetically.

The characteristics of plants are form, texture and color.

The giant forms in native vegetation tend to conform to the natural landforms of that area.

Trees may be used to obstruct awkward angles and lines in the building without distorting other landscaping features.

Berms can successfully make a flat building lot seem more a part of the larger, rolling countryside, effectively making a property seem larger.

Textural coordination between plant materials, building materials, and other non-living landscape elements result in better composition.

Complementary colors in subtle combinations are usually better than stark contrasts that command too much attention.

The more elaborate the trim elements in the building or other structural parts of the landscape, the simpler the design should be, with less contrast in color, texture and form and vice versa. Plant selection should always be based on specifications built during the design process and without consideration of personal prejudices.

Plant selection should begin with only those plants climatically adapted to the area in which they are to be planted.

The moisture retention capabilities, pH, and fertility of a soil determine its capacity for growing healthy plants.

Soil contains minerals, water, humus, living organisms, and air; it is the combination of these elements that determines the soil's suitability for plant growth.

Optimum sun and shade combinations should always be known for plants so that they can be combined with site features, preventing sun related plant injuries and bringing out the best in plant growth, form and color.

That colors change with seasons, alteration interview distance, and amount of light available must be given thought as plants are chosen for color contributions to the landscape.

When it is possible to spread a sequence of blooms throughout the season, color clashes are avoided and blooms have a longer lasting effect on the landscape.

The specific use being made of a plant and the landscape must be considered during its selection. In many cases, the special uses dictate the varieties.

Texture of plant range from fine through course. The stems, leaves, bark create texture and buds and can be seen and felt.

Simplicity, variety, emphasis, balance sequence, and scale are all applied to the composition of a unified landscape planting.

Whenever variable elements are used in a planting unit, emphasis is created. The designer's job is to place greater emphasis where it is warranted.

Good balance may be either symmetrical or asymmetrical. Balance must exist not only from side to side also from foreground to background of view.

As planting units are designed, all possible viewing angles should be considered. The principles of composition must apply for typical viewing points as well as when moving through the landscape.

A point of emphasis in a planting unit is often called a focal point. It may be created by means of an accent plant, a specimen plant serving as accent plant, a hard element, or landscape embellishment.

To control a landscape design, each unit must be designed within itself, since the viewer is incapable of viewing the whole, but units must also relate favorably to one another to tie the landscape together.

Trying design ideas simultaneously in elevation view and plant view is a good way for the designer to form accurate mental images. Plants should be represented at mature size.

Individual plants may have qualities that make them suitable for accenting, massing or as specimen plants standing alone.

Designing in elevation and plan simultaneously without considering individual plant varieties result in the building of a set of plant specifications without prejudice for favorite varieties.

Though buildings can be designed to match their surroundings better, often the landscape designer must work with mismatched architecture.

Elevation drawings are helpful, as the designer can use them to overlay building features with projected landscape concepts.

A focal point may be created at an entryway by a sequence of color or texture or both. Embellishments may be used for accent, or ground pattern lines may direct attention appropriately.

Chapter 4:   What Tools Should Not Be Missing for The Care of My Garden

We all want to consider the outdoors and nature as a fun and relaxing place, which it can be, but it is also a very brutal place with little mercy for the unsuspecting. Most people who think gardening gear is overrated likely haven't experienced one of the many surprises Mother Nature has waiting for you.

Fungus, bacteria, and parasites are all present in the garden along with large and small, venomous creatures. The most common critters, spiders and ants, already give reason enough to wear proper gear.

So, what exactly should you be wearing (or at least consider wearing)? I'll list them and their usefulness.

Gloves - The staple of every gardener. Having your hands protected not only safeguard against potential injuries but also gives you peace at mind that you won't get hurt touching something. Puncture wounds in the garden can be very serious and even the tiniest ones, like those caused by rose thorns, can introduce microbes that cause infections. You can get soft gardening gloves that mainly protect against dirt or you can get heavy-duty gloves, usually called thorn-proof, that protect against physical damage as well as dirt.

Wide-brim Hat and Long Sleeves - I know getting that garden tan might seem like a good thing but the longer you are outside, the more important it becomes to protect yourself from UV damage. I see too many gardeners underestimate the accumulative effect of daily sun exposure. Also, because the effects are often gradual, people don't even notice they are happening until it is overly apparent. Use a large hat and long-sleeve clothing to protect your skin when you plan to be outdoors for several hours.

Bug Repellent - I know you are probably getting a chuckle out of this, but hear me out. Normally, if we go outside and there are too many annoying bugs, we just go back inside. However, the garden doesn't wait for anyone. Sometimes there is no choice but to stay outside and if that's the case, gnats and mosquitoes can quickly drive you crazy. Having some bug repellent is critical for maintaining comfort when gardening. In the cases of mosquitoes, it also helps to preserve your health.

Urban gardeners probably won't need bug repellent but rural gardeners will enjoy the relief it can bring. Keep in mind that I'm not saying to spray yourself every time you go outside. Only use it when the bug pressure is unbearable.

Water-resistant Footwear - This problem varies, but for me, being out in the early morning when the dew is still lingering means my shoes will get soaked after a few minutes of walking around. The moisture can stay in your shoe after you take them off and increase the risk of foot fungus. Soil getting inside your shoe can cause even worse problems if there are open wounds on your feet. That's why it's also important to make sure the footwear you choose is also comfortable.

If you don't want to buy new shoes, you can help prevent fungal issues if your shoes get wet by putting baking soda in them.

Bypass Hand Pruners - Think of pruners as protective gear for your plants. Removing parts of plants to keep the garden healthy is a regular part of the hobby. However, if done with the incorrect equipment, you could do more harm than good. Pruners are designed to make clean cuts that heal better. Improper cuts that can occur from using other objects like scissors not only fail to heal, but can allow fungi and bacteria to enter the plant. Most scissors will lose effectiveness the moment a plant's tissue begins to strengthen. Even non-woody plants can become too tough for scissors to make a clean cut.

There are certainly a lot more pieces of equipment and items that a gardener can find handy, but these are my essentials. There's no reason to go all out with high-priced gimmicks unless you really like them or believe they will truly be worth the money.

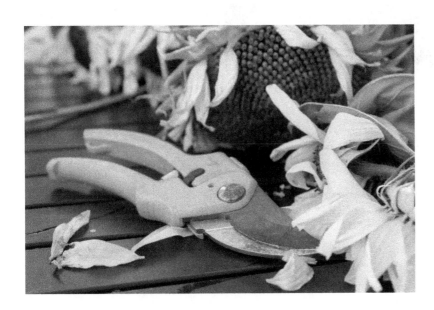

Chapter 5:   Preparing the Soil for Planting

Soil science is a complicated field of study that encompasses the sciences of chemistry, hydrology, microbiology, physics, biology, and ecology. Sometimes soil scientists are irritated by those who call soil "dirt" because the noun dirt implies a lifeless, stagnant physical medium. The truth is actually quite the opposite; soil is a dynamic, living, and constantly changing ecological community. The key to a great garden is the quality of the soil. Avid gardeners know that by continuously improving their garden soil, they are ensuring a productive garden for years to come.

Beneficial Roles of Soil

Soil serves many vital roles: it functions as a medium for plant growth, it is a recycler of raw materials, it operates as an environmental filter, it aids in the regulation of water supplies, it provides habitat for soil organisms, and it performs as an engineering medium. Without soil, our planet could not support most life! Humans also depend on soil; plants use nutrients from the soil to produce the food that we consume. Therefore, understanding the needs of healthy soil is an important first step toward growing a successful garden. For those with limited knowledge of soil, here is a brief overview of introductory concepts of soil science.

Soil Texture

Soil texture is described as the relative proportion or percent of three particles: sand, silt, and clay. Figure 25, soil texture triangle, illustrates the relationship between particle size distribution and soil texture classes. A major misconception is that the percent of organic matter is described in soil textures. This is incorrect. Although organic matter is an important component of soils, it does not contribute to soil texture. Differences between sand, silt, and clay particles are most simply described by their relative sizes.

Most soils contain a mixture of sand, silt, and clay particles but may be dominated by one particle type. A dominating particle type can determine properties of the soil such as water infiltration and nutrient retention. Reference Topsoil Quality Guidelines for Landscaping for a summary of topsoil quality guidelines.

Sand

Sand, the largest particle size (2–0.05 millimeters in diameter), can be seen by the naked eye and has a gritty texture when rubbed between two fingers. Sand is a physical component of the soil. Without a binding agent, sand particles do not stick together, and water and minerals in the soil are not attracted to sand particles. Therefore, sand particles do not tend to provide plants with adequate nutrients. Think of a beach. Are plants prolific on sandy beaches? Although some exceptions exist, most plants will not thrive in sand-dominated growing mediums unless the medium is amended with organic matter and/or supplied with nutrients. Sand does provide excellent drainage for plants. Most plants are not adapted to conditions where roots are growing in stagnant water. Again, some exceptions exist like plants adapted for wetland conditions, but typically poorly draining soils or constantly saturated conditions are stressful on plant growth. Sanddominated soils prevent this stress by rapidly draining water from the plant's root-zone; consequently, sand-dominated soils require more frequent watering and fertilization applications for adequate plant growth. Sand-

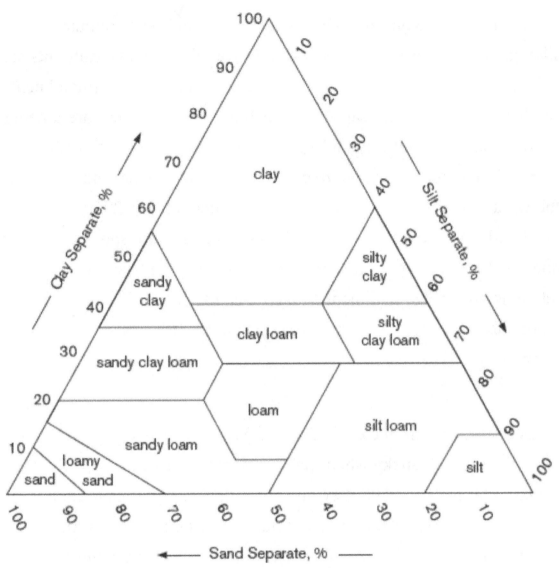

dominated soil textures include sand and loamy sand. Soil

texture triangle

Silt

Silt, the second largest particle size (0.05–0.002 millimeters in diameter), is not visible to the naked eye. Silt particles feel smooth but not sticky when wet and rubbed between fingers. Silt particles have a somewhat higher water holding capacity than sand; however, silt-dominated soil textures are improved with the addition of organic matter. Because silt particles are only moderately attracted to one another, organic matter aids silt-dominated soils in building soil structure. Silt soils have a low ability to retain nutrients so, typically, silt should not be considered a sole soil amendment. Amendments with higher nutrient holding capacities, such as organic matter, are a better option to increase soil fertility. When dry, silt appears powdery with some clods. Silt is commonly transported via water in streams and rivers or windblown as loess. Of current interest is the Illinois River 2020 project in which silt is being dredged from the Illinois River and transported to other locations to be used for habitat restoration projects and landscapes. The project aims to dredge sediment-filled parts of the river for improved recreation use and fish and wildlife populations (Illinois River Project Overview).

Clay

Clay (less than 0.002 millimeters in diameter) is the smallest of the three-soil particle sizes and feels sticky when wet. Soil samples that can be formed into a ball, like Play-Doh®, when they are moist have a significant amount of clay. Clay has high water retention and nutrient adsorptive properties. This means clay-dominated soils have a tendency to hold onto water and nutrients for prolonged periods. A major misconception among the public is that clay soils are "bad" or "infertile." Many Utahns are tempted to start fresh by bringing in outside topsoil or building raised beds to avoid planting in claydominated soils. While these options are certainly possible, clay-dominated soils can be amended overtime with organic matter to provide an excellent garden soil. Remember, clay-dominated soils tend to hold on to nutrients; therefore, amended soils serve as an excellent bank of essential nutrients for plant growth requirements.

Loam

Loam soils are a composition of sand, silt, and clay percentages that form an ideal plant-growing medium. Loam soils are a best-case scenario; loam soils provide adequate drainage, water retention, and nutrient adsorptive properties for ideal plant growth. Nationally, most soils are loams although loam soils may be dominated by a particular soil particle size such as sandy loam, silt loam, or clay loam. Although loam soils are considered ideal garden soils, loam soils still benefit from the addition of organic matter. Soil texture can be determined by feel; however, the simplest and most accurate way to determine soil texture is to have soil tested by the local land-grant university soil testing laboratory. Soil texture can also be determined by viewing the Web Soil Survey online (USDA-NRCS Web Soil Survey). No matter how soil texture is determined, most gardeners hope that the results show that they live in loam Ville! Loam soils include: loam, fine sandy loam, very fine sandy loam, silt loam, sandy clay loam, and silty clay loam.

Soil Testing

Although differences in soil textures might seem obvious from the descriptions above, correctly identifying a soil texture by feel takes the expertise of a trained professional. Fortunately, having soil tested by a professional is both inexpensive and convenient. USU Extension recommends having soil tested for those planning a garden or experiencing problems growing fruits and vegetables. It is ideal to have soil tested by the local land-grant university because the tests performed and recommendations provided are adapted to a specific growing area and tend to be significantly less expensive than a private soil testing laboratory. Tests range from a basic analysis (phosphorus and potassium only) to a complete analysis (pH, salinity, texture, phosphorus, potassium, nitrate-nitrogen, micronutrients, sulfate, and organic matter). For gardeners on a budget, USU Extension usually recommends a routine soil analysis (pH, salinity, texture, phosphorus, potassium), and recommendations from the soil testing technician on advised nutrient additions.

Soil pH

Soil pH impacts gardening plans because variations in pH affect plant nutrient availability and soil microorganism activity. The pH scale ranges from 0 to 14 with 7 being neutral. Values above 7.0 are considered alkaline and pH values below 7.0 are considered acidic. Utah soils tend to be slightly alkaline with pH values of 7.5 to 8.5. Fortunately, pH values in this range are suitable for production of most fruit and vegetable crops; however, some pH sensitive crops, such as berries and grapes, may show signs of nutrient deficiencies. Phosphorus, iron, manganese, molybdenum, copper, boron, and zinc deficiencies are possible with soil pH values above 7.5. Soil pH values above 8.2 make it difficult to grow some crops. Check with your local Extension office if your soil test results measure above this pH value.

Soil Salinity

Salinity is a measure of the soluble salts in the soil. Saline soils are not the same as sodic soils. Sodic soil properties are dominated by an excess of exchangeable sodium (Na); while saline soils contain high levels of salts of other cations, like magnesium and calcium. High salinity concentrations inhibit seed germination of sensitive plants and can suppress growth due to increased water stress. Such stress is sometimes referred to as "chemical drought" because affected plants look as if they are suffering from lack of water. Fortunately, it is possible to move salt away from the root zone of garden plants. Soluble salts can be leached or washed from the soil during extended irrigation. Water should be added to the soil surface in one continuous irrigation event over an extended period of time. The idea is that water will super-saturate the soil, dissolve soluble salts, and push the salts down through the soil and away from the rooting-zone of plants. As a general reference, to leach soil with good internal drainage, apply:

6 inches of water to cut salts by 50 percent

12 inches of water to cut salts by 80 percent

24 inches of water to cut salts by 90 percent

Soil Compaction

One of a gardener's worst enemies is soil compaction. Soil compaction is where the soil structure is destroyed through one or more of many causes: construction, significant foot or vehicle traffic, frequent travel patterns from animals like dogs, or placement of heavy loads on an area of soil. Compacted soil lacks adequate pore space for air and water movement through the soil, and acts as a barrier against plant roots exploring surrounding soil for water and nutrients.

Therefore, plants typically struggle to remain healthy under compacted conditions. Clay-dominated soils are especially susceptible to soil compaction as are wet soils. Therefore, it is best to avoid construction or tilling soils that are moist or saturated with water.

Compaction can be alleviated in affected areas through multiple techniques. Aerating the compacted area with a hollow tine aerator will help reintroduce water and air movement to the root zone of plants. Garden areas can be rototilled. Compaction can also be alleviated through the incorporation of organic matter. Avoid placing heavy items in your garden area. It is wise to strategically place stepping stones in the garden so compaction is limited to a few pre-planned areas. Consider how people will move through the garden and design walkways or pathways to accommodate this natural flow of foot traffic.

Chapter 6:   Rock Garden for Landscaping

Definition of a Rocky Garden:

A rocky garden is a garden that reflects nature with a rough surface that is not level, with the presence of a rock element in the same form as it is found in nature in its irregular shape in terms of size, distribution and growth of plants in the form of groups.

The element of rocks prevails over the rest of the design elements in this type of garden. The rock garden is an area of land, whether flat or uneven (by adding soil to it) to grow some plants that do not need continuous follow-up with the presence of rocks, which is the basis of their design.

The purposes of establishing the rock garden:

1- In addition to the aesthetic purpose of designing the rocky garden, it isalso for the purpose of obtaining diversity in the accepted forms of gardens and thus adding an element of suspense to them by reflecting on them to discover new elements in relation to the traditional garden elements.

2- These gardens are also resorted to when there is no good knowledge ofthe origins of agriculture and how to take care of the gardens.

3- Among the other reasons behind its presence among the various types ofgardens due to the lack of natural environment for the ingredients of agriculture: high temperatures, lack of irrigation water resources, unevenness of the earth's surface.

It is worth noting that the rocky garden plants are of a nature that makes them endure the harsh environment conditions, and despite that, these plants have attractive and different shapes and colors at the same time.

Rock Garden Specifications:

1- One or two types of rocks are used in one garden until they have credibility in their simulations of nature, where the rocks of one region are available in the form of two or two types at most (such as granite rocks with marble rocks).

2- Coordination of rocks in an orderly and not random way, because naturehas large rocks at the top and then smaller ones at the bottom. The modern wide part is partially buried in the ground and the old part is visible due to exposure to erosion factors in addition to burying the broken parts as well.

3- The place of the garden be exposed to the sun throughout the day.

4- The roof on which the rock garden is chosen is an uneven surface, preferably with a gradient slope.

5- The garden soil is sandy with good drainage.

6- A third of the rocks are buried in the soil and not placed directly on thesoil surface.

7- The placement of rocks, the broad ones of which are horizontal, not distressed or tilted and in contact with the soil.

8- A water element can be used, such as a fountain or a small waterfall fromwhich water flows between rocks.

9- Place a layer of grit or break the stone with a thickness of 10-15 cmbefore laying the soil soil layer for drainage.

10- Defining the garden area with an industrial or natural fence (with astructural or vegetable fence).

11- Types of plants used in the rock garden, some of which are the followingtypes:

Herbs: lavender, thyme, selafia, mint.

Flowering plants: violet, narcissus, tulip.

Trees and shrubs: pine, garonia, etc.

12- Arranging flowers:

Depending on the flowering season, the plants that bloom in the spring are planted next to the ones that bloom in the summer, then the ones that bloom in the fall, so that the garden is blooming throughout the year.

Depending on the color of the flowers, the contrast system is used to arrange the colors, or the flowers that are not related to the color are placed next to each other, as white is next to blue or pink, and green is next to red or orange.

Types of Rock Gardens:

There are four types of rock gardens:

1- The mountain or the rock garden that is established on slopes:

The sloping garden is the one that takes a sloping shape, and this slope in the ground is either available naturally or an artificial slope is made by placing the appropriate soil to do this. Gradient, with removal of a layer of soil in all areas with a depth of not less than 30 cm.

It is possible to make lanes or steps to connect between different levels of this garden.

Plants are planted on the evergreen top of trees, then herbaceous plants in group form. 2- Wall Garden:

The rock wall garden is built on the wall of the walls by lining the natural stones on one row, leaving between them spaces, then the soil and plants are placed without pressure on them, then the next row is pressed over it and so on.

It is possible to stack all layers of stones first and upon completion the plants are planted as a final stage. Cement materials are not used to compact stones, but their adhesion depends on their weight. The choice should be made for specific herbal plants.

3- Botanical garden:

This garden can be implemented in one of the corners of the house, provided that the choice is located on a sunny location for it, but in this case the ponds are built with the following specifications:

The height of the basin is not less than 60 cm in a location close to the places of sitting.

The material of the materials used in building the walls of the house is the same as those used in building the basin.

The width of the basin should not be more than 1 meter or less.

Make holes in the bottom of the basin to drain the excess water from the plants.

For a good drainage, place a 10-15 cm depth.

Choosing 3-4 different size stones of one type, and one third of the stone is buried in the soil at least.

Long plants are grown in size, then shorter and shorter, whereas the sagging ones are at the edge of the basin.

Some small or oversized rocks are placed on the surface of the soil or in any corner of the basin to cover the areas in it.

4- Garden of Ponds:

The advantage of this mini garden is that it can be moved from one place to another as desired due to its appropriate size that can be carried by the person, and it has two methods of cultivation:

The first method:

Using a large-sized limestone stone that is placed over the surface of the soil, then a cavity is made in this stone Naturally shaped, with a depth of at least 25-30 cm. The cavity is filled with agricultural soil, and then cultivate one or two species at most in this cavity.

The second method:

Using a large plate or basin with holes in its bottom to drain the water in excess of the plant's need. The sides of the basin are covered with a paste of cement, sand and pitmos in 1: 1: 2 ratios, then the basin is filled with prepared soil.

3-4 large irregular stones are chosen to be planted in the sink and a third are buried, and grit can be added to cover the surface. This pond is suitable for planting some conical shrubs and herbaceous plants. The basin is also placed above the soil surface.

Chapter 7: Using Plants for Colors and Textures

Color is one of the most important components in landscape design. There are at least six types of color schemes that can be used to plan your garden and each refers to positions on the color wheel. When discussing colors, the terminology "warm" refers to colors that are on the right side of the color wheel (reds, oranges and yellows) and "cool" colors refer to those on the left (blues, greens and purples). If you are looking for the most impact when combining colors, use complementary colors, those which are on opposite sides of the color wheel. Examples of complementary colors are purple and yellow, blue and orange, or green and red. In each case, one color adds to the intensity of the opposite, supplying the most contrast in the garden.

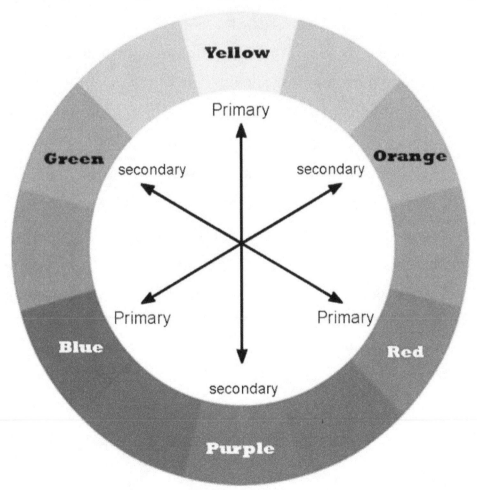

Landscape Design Color Wheel Photo Credit: Cornell ed.

"Warm" colors refer to those that are on the right of the color wheel (reds, oranges and yellows) and "cool" colors are those on the left side of the color wheel (blues, greens and purples)

Other combinations can be monochromic, analogous, primary, pastel, harmonious, or riotous. The meaning of monochromic refers to a grouping of plants of the same color, such as in a "moon garden", which is composed of all white blooms that bring brightness to a garden setting at night. Various tones of the same color can also be used in a monochromic setting, such as bright pink and soft pink or bright yellow and muted yellow. Colors also tend to fall into two categories. Dark colors (blues, purples, deep pinks) create a more calming and serene effect and tend to make areas look larger, while light colors (reds, oranges, yellows) tend to draw attention and make a space look smaller.

From a distance the colors may appear the same, but in a closer view, there is a rich mix of color that is visually harmonious. Either a warm or cool effect can be created, depending on the choice of colors selected.

Primary colors are those colors that are can be combined to create a large array of other colors and hues. There are three basic primary colors, those of red, yellow and blue.

When used in their original form, they often create a very bold statement and are used to attract attention and stimulate the senses. Large botanical gardens often use these bold colors together to create a dramatic effect for their visitors. When the use of only primary colors together is a bit too stimulating, the use of shades or tints of each color can be used along with them to create a more softening touch.

While bright colors energize the garden, pastels or muted colors are those used to create a peaceful and tranquil setting. Pastels such as soft pinks, lavender and peach look best in the front of a shady border, while bright colors such as red, bright yellow, orange and magenta draw lots of attention to a sunny spot. Pastel colors combine best with other pastel colors and look best when combined with plants that have either silvery or white foliage.

The last category is the use of a riotous color scheme, or the use of multiple bold colors together. This combination creates the sense of an energetic garden which is visually stimulating.

When combining several colors, it is best to use masses of each color and plant in repetition to create unity and flow.

When it comes to foliage, green is considered a neutral color, or one that can be used without changing the effect of the others. Shades of brown, black, grey, silver and white are also considered to be neutral. Variegated foliage consisting of shades

Sample designs with color combinations for you to use as a guideline.

Color Combination for Continuous Spring-Fall Interest

In this driveway pier planting is Coreopsis 'Zagreb' with Nepeta 'Walkers Low' (in the backdrop to the left). The combination of complementary colors yellow and blue (yellow Coreopsis) with (blue Nepeta) makes for an outstanding display of color throughout the entire warm weather season. The display is complemented by Golden Oriental Spruce 'Skylands' (center left), an evergreen which adds beautiful golden foliage throughout every season. Coreopsis and Nepeta are winter hardy to USDA plant hardiness zone 3 and 'Skylands' Spruce is hardy to USDA zone 5.

Color Combination Spring-Fall

In this design, blue-green Weeping Blue Atlas Cedar (Cedrus atlantica 'Pendula') is bordered on each side by burgundy Barberry 'Rosy Glow'. Also included is golden evergreen Chamaecyparis 'Gold Mop', springblooming purple perennial Salvia 'May Night', summer blooming Heuchera 'Caramel' (right of Gold Mop Cypress) and in center front is late summerfall blooming Dwarf Butterfly Bush Lo & Behold 'Blue Chip'. (Note) If Barberry has been declared as invasive in your area, alternatives for burgundy foliage include Weigela 'Wine and Roses' and Ninebark 'Diabolo'.

Dwarf Butterfly Bush (Zones 5-9)

Caramel Coral Bells (Zone 4-9)

Salvia 'May Night' (Zones 4-9)

'Gold Mop' Cypress (Zones 5-7)

Weeping Blue Atlas Cedar (Zones 6-9)

Barberry 'Rosy Glow' (Zones 4-8)

Complementary Colors

Combine opposite sides of the color wheel. Seen here are perennials Coreopsis 'Zagreb' (yellow blooms) with Nepeta 'Walkers Low' (bluishpurple blooms) in the backdrop. The contrasting colors of purple and yellow create a dramatic look in the landscape. Coreopsis grows 12-18 inches tall and is hardy in USDA zones 3-9, with blooms from early summer until fall. Nepeta (backdrop) grows to a taller 24-36 inches tall, is hardy in USDA zones 3-8 and blooms from summer into fall. Both plants require full sun to partial shade, moderate watering and a well-drained soil.

Montgomery Globe Spruce and 'Stella D Oro' Daylily make the perfect combination of evergreen with perennial. The bright blue hue of Montgomery Blue Globe Spruce is ongoing throughout the entire year, while the bright yellow blooms of Stella D' Oro Daylily complement it throughout the growing season. Montgomery Globe Spruce is hardy in USDA zones 28, prefers full sun to partial shade and a well-drained soil. It grows to a mature height of 3-4 feet tall by 3 feet wide. Daylily 'Stella D Oro' is hardy in USDA zones 4-11, prefers full sun to partial shade and a well-drained soil, and grows to a height of 24-30 inches tall by 12-24 inches wide. Repeat blooms are displayed throughout summer and into fall.

The soft white foliage of Lamb's Ear (Stachys) is even more prominent when combined with either the dark purple blooms of salvia or bright pink blooms of Chinese Astilbe 'Visions'. All three plants are hardy in USDA zones 4-9. While Lamb's Ear and Salvia prefer full sun to partial shade, Astilbe prefers partial to full shade, but thrives when given the proper irrigation and massed with the taller Stachys.

The combination starts off with purple Salvia 'May Night', which takes flower in late spring, followed by the bright yellow, flat blooms of Yarrow 'Moonshine'. The two will bloom throughout much of the summer together, and as the Salvia reaches the end of its bloom cycle, the yarrow will hold the fort down. With deadheading of the salvia, both plants will supply a colorful combination all summer. Below is a combination of May Night Salvia with Japanese Golden Sedge in the backdrop. The same color combination of purple and gold work together to complement the landscape.

Chapter 8:   Garden Landscape Ideas

Mulch, Rocks and Pavers

Accenting your landscape is almost as important as the plants you choose. There are so many ways to neaten up the look of your yard, using mulch, stones, pavers, or crushed seashells. You have to decide what the function will be of your soil covering. Are you looking for great drainage? Weed deterrent? Aesthetic look only? There are many reasons to choose any given soil covering so we will look at the top 3: mulch, rocks, and pavers.

There are so many varieties of mulch to choose from, and they have different colors as well as different scents. Some good reasons to choose mulch is they help retain moisture for the plants, deter weeds from growing, keep the temperature moderate in retaining warmth in the ground, and control soil erosion.

It can add a lovely accent to your flower beds and around your shrubs and trees. There are no real disadvantages to using mulch, with exception that is you live in a year-round warm climate, small animals such as voles can make your mulch bed their home. To deter that from happening, a light raking once a week should prevent the critters from moving in.

Rocks and stones are an elegant addition to any garden. There are a million different types from which to choose, so it all depends on your preference. Using stones in your garden requires minimal maintenance and they do not decay, which prevents insects from inhabiting your yard. They are attracted to decaying wood, so using stone is a great option to keep the bugs out. The drawbacks of using stone are that no nutrients decay to feed the plants with and they retain heat and lose it quickly so the temperature flux can affect sensitive plants. They can also sink into the soil over time, which can change the pH composition of the garden. They do also offer excellent drainage, ensuring all the plants get water to the roots.

If you don't want to go all rocks in the garden, they can still add a lovely decorative touch by using them as borders, denoting the start of a garden bed. Also, they are perfect for footpaths, which can protect your grass from being treaded on daily.

Lastly, pavers are a great option for a cool decorative look, and they are great weed deterrents. However, they do not offer much in the way of allowing drainage, but they do an excellent job keeping the soil from eroding. The best use of pavers is in combination with mulch or stone. This way you can get the best of both worlds, depending on the look and style you want to achieve. The most elegant walkways are created with pavers, and they are not overly expensive.

No matter which material you choose, it is sure to add a beautiful touch to your yard, and add curb appeal to your home.

Garden Styles

With your grass growing green, and your soil cover chosen, you will of course want to start picking flowers and décor additions for your landscape. First, it is important to nail down a style you want to carry through your yard. No matter what type of home you have, you can pretty much do anything you want in your yard. However, if you chose a lovely old Victorian as you homestead, I would venture to guess you love that style so perhaps an English garden would be ideal for you. It is all a matter of taste and preferences. We are going to discuss four different styles, though there are many more for you to research.

Creating a landscape to look like the Old West is very simple, and can be lots of fun! The Southwest style can range from western looks to Native

American feel. Choosing earthy colors such as Navajo red and earthy greens, maybe a splash of blue can add so much to your landscape. Plants can include cactus, agave, or yucca. Using clay pots, hand painted by Native Americans is a beautiful touch.

In the case of the Southwest style, less is more. Remember, you are recreating a desert look, so use of stones and rocks is excellent, as well as low shrubs. Stay in the earth tone palette, and you too can have an awesome throwback yard that is easy to maintain.

The English garden is a traditional favorite. With accents of lattice work and wrought iron, the elegant flowers of an English garden add style to any landscape. Using colors in the pastel family, coupled with antique pink hydrangea or vibrant yellow forsythia, bring out the traditional look you love. Perfectly clipped hedges can be used to create little compartments within your yard, giving you little pockets of privacy and quiet reading nooks. Lavish displays of riotous flowers, like the ever-popular impatiens, make the English garden an eye-catching landscape, even from across the neighborhood.

Another favorite landscape style is Asian or Zen, using minimal décor and flowers to create a peaceful yard in which to relax. The style offers an environment that invites mediation and contemplation, using natural stone and hand shaped plants. Think bonsai, but on a grander scale. Create paths that meander, not go directly to the home, as it is said in Asian culture that evil or mischievous spirits are fooled my paths that zigzag, while they will come straight into the home if they are designed so. Use the view from your home to create your focal points in the yard. Look out various windows and see where their sight lines land, and there should be your beautiful Asian art accents, like a Buddha statue, or plant a dwarf Japanese maple.

Bamboo and rocks are lovely editions to any Zen garden.

Lastly, the modern style landscape is another option from which to choose. Using clean lines and vibrant color combinations, this style is best suited for those who love bold design and geometrical shapes. Inspired by colors and style from the 50's and 60's, a modern landscape is feels very organized. The focus tends to be more on hardscapes than plants, using furniture, stone, and the home for style structure. Splashes of color are used to round out the look, and offer a fun atmosphere. Other materials used to create the modern landscape are cement and various metals.

There are many more designs than just the four I have touched upon here. If something hasn't struck your fancy, then be sure to keep researching. Perhaps the Tuscan look suits you better or perhaps French. These selections are a sampling of a much greater list for you from which to choose. Pick what works best for you and what you and your family will love to spend weekend afternoons enjoying for years to come.

Chapter 9:   Climate for Landscape

A year-round garden is one that has interest all through the year – not only when the flowers are blooming, but in all seasons, even in winter. There's always something interesting going on in the year-round garden, and that's the appeal of it. Creating such a garden is a challenge, but a fun one.

I really do love perennials, the workhorses of the garden. You can find a number of old-fashioned plants that can last for years and years and use them to make a long-lived garden. But if you want a good, all-season garden, mix in other kinds of plants, such as shrubs, annuals, vines, bulbs, ornamental grasses, and even small trees.

The best way to make a year-round garden is to choose plants, when possible, that provide interest for more than one season. So, you'd find plants that not only have beautiful flowers, but they also offer fall color, or variegated leaves, or a striking form, or winter berries. In fact, the plant doesn't even have to flower, in the traditional sense of the term, if you plant a bed of striking ferns, or punctuate your garden with stands of ornamental grasses.

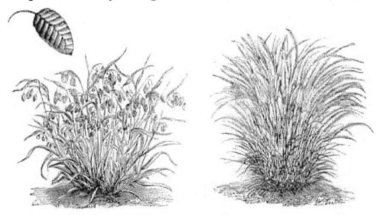

Northern sea oats (Chasmanthium latifolium) and fountaingrass (Pennisetum spp.)

These plant choices add color, form, beauty, and seasonal interest, and help fill in gaps of time when only one or two of your perennials are blooming –

which happens, especially when you're just started your garden and haven't gotten all your plants synced up yet.

The key here is to mix your flowers with other elements to give your garden form, a sense of composition, but also color and interest that carries your outdoor landscape through the whole year. Even if you go out in winter, you'll still have elements in your garden that catch your eye and give you something pleasing to look at – a twisty, gnarled specimen tree, or bright red berries, each capped with snow, or a series of red-twig dogwood shrubs all looking merry against the white land, or a paperbark maple with its colorful exfoliating sienna bark.

And if you've under planted your plants with bulbs in early spring, you can have flowers such as scilla and snowdrops and crocuses even before the snow cover is gone, before your other plants are even up and blooming.

There are a number of things you can add to the garden to give it interest all year around. Your palette is as varied as the kinds of plants you can buy.

Read on for good plant selections for each season to try in your year-round garden.

Spring

Spring is the excitement season. This is especially true after you've gone through a snowy blah winter where the whole world is white and brown and gray, and it's dark when you leave work every night, and all you get is endless gloom and cold outside. I should add that it's winter right now as I'm writing this. I have been wearing a coat constantly for the last three months, and nobody lets you hibernate if you're not a bear. It's a damn shame.

Anyway, spring is the excitement season when all the fresh green comes up and everything warms up and the spring birds come back and start building nests. And the sun is out in the spring! The wonderful warm sun!

But there's not a lot blooming in your garden in early spring, so that's when you need to add in some good spring plants to get the season started.

Trees

Early spring blooming trees include redbuds and witch hazel. Witch hazel trees, Hamamelis spp., bloom very early in the year, its flowers making an appearance when you're still wearing 13 layers and shivering in front of the space heater. But at least you can look outside and see the crinkly little yellow witch hazel flowers and say "Spring's almost here!" Witch hazel is a low-maintenance, native tree that tops out at 10 to 20 feet.

Shrubs

Early spring blooming shrubs include old favorites like forsythia. These are now available in longer blooming varieties with brighter yellow flowers.

Pieris, also known as andromeda (Pieris formosa var. forrestii), is a shrub I kept meaning to add to various gardens, but for one reason or another never managed to do. These make an excellent show in spring. The new leaves on this plant come out bright red, fading to pink, then white, then green. The leaves almost look like flowers themselves. It makes for quite a show.

In spring – in some places, as early as March – Pieris bursts into bloom with drooping panicles of fragrant white or pink flowers that look like tiny lanterns. This shrub does prefer acidic soil, but if you can grow a magnolia tree in your yard, then you can grow a Pieris. Mulch it with a deep layer of peat or pine needles.

Bulbs and corms

Early-blooming bulbs such as snowdrops, crocuses, Siberian squill, with tiny flowers in the most wonderful shade of cerulean, and daffodils will help you get a jump on spring.

Tulips are one of the classic flowers of spring, and they're available in so many different varieties, species, and forms. You can get the Greigii hybrids, which have reddish-purple lines on the upper leaves and large, cuplike flowers with an eye at the center; or the small Tulips tarda, which bears clusters of four or five starry flowers. Some tulips can be planted as longlived perennials. Others, such as the exquisite 'Angelique,' which look like ruffled pink peonies, will need to be treated as annuals and replaced every year.

Summer

Trees

I used to write for a website that sold plants in the deep south, and Vitex agnus-castus, known as chaste tree, was an especially noteworthy tree that sold very well there. And for good reason: Vitex is a small, multi-stemmed tree with panicles of sweetly-scented purple blossoms. The green-grey foliage, too, is scented. This little tree gets only 10 to 20 feet tall, so it's easy to tuck it into your yard where you want its fragrance and color. Vitex doesn't need much maintenance, though you'll have to trim off shoots so the tree won't turn into a shrub. (Of course, if you are so inclined you can certainly let it go shrubby.) Apparently, the Vitex is also hardy up to zone 5, so I hope to see more of it in my area.

Shrubs

In the wild, elderberries (Sambucus nigra) are good shrubs for birds, bearing a profusion of large platters of tiny white flowers, followed by small purpleblack berries that are edible for birds and people alike (though quite seedy). I pick the berry clusters and put them in the chicken yard as treats for my hens. However, wild elderberries also spread like crazy via seeds and suckers, and is often scraggly.

Perennials

Ornamental grasses are good candidates for the all-seasons garden. They provide form, long-lasting color, and winter interest while being hardy and carefree.

Hakonechola is one example of an ornamental grass that really fits the bill. It's a lovely grass from Japan, where its beauty is greatly prized. It's a low, mounded grass, variegated yellow and green, and in fall produces feathery flower plumes.

Fall

Trees

Most every deciduous tree is a winner in fall. Sugar maples, white and green ash trees, red maples, sweet gum trees all deck themselves in gorgeous colors. What's more, all of these trees have new hybrids and selections on the market, all of which are bred for really intense, reliable color.

Black gum, or tupelo, Nyssa sylvatica, is one such tree. Tupelo is a very slow-growing tree, but its leaves turn a most amazing hue of scarlet in autumn.

Shrubs

Chokeberry, Aronia arbutifolia, bears fragrant white to light-pink flowers in spring. In fall, chokeberry trees bear a generous portion of brilliant red berries that last through the winter (and you can make jam or jelly with them). When you add in its epic, brilliant red fall color, chokecherry makes a great year-round shrub. This shrub can spread to some extent, but it's a great low-maintenance plant and looks good in naturalized masses in borders or natural settings. It is a member of the rose family, which is why its spring flowers resemble apple blossoms.

Perennials

Asters are an old favorite, though in some areas they can be an invasive species. But they come in so many different sizes, shapes, and colors, that you can create a huge drift of them by siting tall asters in the back down to dwarf aster varieties in the front. Asters are carefree and don't need much care and really can put on a show of color.

Winter

Trees

Specimens with exfoliating bark are a good choice for year-round beauty, but they make an especially good show in winter. River birch (Betula nigra) is a great, multi-stemmed tree with buff-colored peeling bark. It's a good shade tree through summer and has plenty of winter interest. Also, it's resistant to borers, which paper birch trees (including European white birch, Betula papyrifera) tend to be susceptible to.

Shrubs

For winter interest, choose shrubs with interesting bark or colorful twigs (as with the red-twig dogwoods) and berries. Bonus points planting shrubs with berries that birds enjoy eating. Cedar waxwings seem to like honeysuckle berries.

Evergreen shrubs through the garden will help keep some green, or at least greenish colors, in your garden even when snow is thick on the ground. Plant some little boxwoods, trimmed into balls, through the garden to keep the design lively.

Ornamental grasses

Add ornamental grasses to your winter garden. These come in all kinds of different forms and shapes. Hakonechloa, also known as Japanese forestgrass, is a yellow and green weeping grass. Blue fescue is small and spiky and bluish and cute. Pennisetum is about two or three feet tall with wine-red leaves and soft red foxtails. You don't have to trim back your ornamental grasses in fall – keep them to provide winter interest in your garden.

Flowers in winter?! Sure!

In late fall, you can plant some cold-loving flowers and plants to carry your landscape into winter. Pansies are the ultimate warriors when the temperature drops, and will keep smiling even as the snow's falling on them.

Ornamental kale is also cold-hardy, and will brighten a landscape through November and even December, depending on weather.

Chapter 10: Landscaping with Trees

Landscape Gardening is all about creating a space that fits your tastes and needs. If you hire a garden designer to do the job for you, there is an additional advantage of increasing the value of your house.

You can create a garden landscape filled with colors all year round, with knowledge of trees, bulbs, annuals, perennials and planting themes.

When landscaping their yards so many people prefer trees and this is for many reasons. Let's look at why trees are added not just for beauty but also the other reasons why planting some in your yard could be a great idea.

Above all, Trees bring elegance to a yard. Landscaping with trees adds dimension to a yard and can be focus points while planting in certain areas. They can transform a boring flat yard into one which flows with life and air. Trees will act as a natural barrier, providing neighbors protection when they are planted in a row along the edge of your house. They offer beauty throughout the year, and they have something to give during each season in areas that are going through a climate change.

Spring brings new leaves, new growth and buds, which are a welcome sign of the coming warm weather. Summer is bringing absolute, luscious foliage that many mothers will appreciate. Autumn brings before falling the magic process of the tree's leaves, turning various shades of color. Winter will carry bare trees, but after a snowfall, they look so lovely and are covered with a white blanket.

Apart from the beauty aspect in terms of trees landscaping, many people are opting for fruit trees. That offers beauty and intent for an individual. Fruit trees can be harvested to supplement one's food supply, and many who have multiple trees choose to sell any extra fruit on the side of the road to get some side income. A lot of people find local, fresh fruit very appealing.

Trees are great for shading a house, and wind defense. What fits well in both cold and hot months. Despite trees offering shade during hot months, a homeowner will find that the house will stay considerably cooler as nature provides a natural umbrella. Because of the house, the tree can suck up the sunlight. Often, they can serve as windbreakers, dispersing heavy winds so they don't strike the home as hard as they would otherwise, and this will significantly minimize drafts.

Trees are a perfect way to mark the passing of time, too. Every year you'll enjoy seeing your tree grow and in time, younger generations will enjoy what was once planted long ago. Fruit trees can often take two to three years to harvest, so it's fun to see the tree grow and mature to the point that it offers apples, pears, peaches or other delicious fruits.

Finally, a yard that doesn't have landscaping doesn't appeal to anyone. Planting trees will add value to your land, for that reason. This is particularly true when trees are being established, and a new owner need not worry about staking and other issues. Anyone who decides a property's worth must take into account all aspects, the elegance, the focal points, the shade the trees provide and the protection they can offer.

Chapter 11: Edible Landscape Gardening

If you never considered landscaping edible, now is the time to start! But how do you know that edible landscaping is for you, right? Here are several ways of doing this:

1. Love gardening. There's no real difference when you compare gardeningusing edible plants and gardening using non-edible plants — you still dig and plant, water and weed. It doesn't matter if you cut flowers for your table! Indeed, many of the flowers that you do not find edible, such as daylilies, nasturtium, and pansies, are actually very healthy!

2. You just love eating. If you enjoy cooking, the edible landscape is greatfor you. When you imagine all of your favorite fruits and vegetables, just wait outside to go out and eat... Ok, it sounds like paradise to me!

3. You fancy good food. New is better than home-grown, so you can't getany fresher. You can pick your fruit and vegetables when they are in your own yard at their peak of ripeness and flavor. When you've got edible landscaping, you have full control over what's going into and on your food. No chemicals of mystery in there!

4. You love the convenience of just outside your door to pick food. Youwaste less time in-store lines of edible landscaping, less money on transportation, and have more time, resources and money to waste with your children. You can just step out and get your favorite fruits and vegetables, whenever you like.

5. They love to try new foods. There are so many types of edible plants outthere you'll never run out of fruit and vegetables to try. If you don't enjoy the taste and the plant is beautiful, then no problem — just give away the extra.

If you like it, it's made for you!

6.　You just love cooking. The best chefs swear by their kitchen gardens, andif you're looking to go the next step in your cooking skills, just what you need is an edible landscape. Your cooking can't help but be great with the very freshest, most perfectly ripe fruit and vegetables in the exact varieties that you love!

7.　You love to have a pretty lot. Edible landscaping is not just about puttingfood plants in the front yard — it is about building a landscape on which you can feel proud. It's about making the exterior of your home, not just beautiful but also edible.

Planting and Maintain an Edible Landscape

Edible landscaping means the use of beautiful, food-producing plants in a well-designed garden than the usual ornamental plants. The typical American lawn may provide visual satisfaction but does not feed the people. An edible landscape provides affordable and fresh foods, various blooming plants, constantly changing surroundings, and a home for butterflies, birds and bees. It can be created in whatever style and can be incorporated with mixing ornamental and edible plants.

It is the least understood kind of landscaping. An edible landscape provides an alternative to conventional landscapes that are exclusively designed for ornamental purposes. Edible landscaping includes shrubs and trees that bear fruit and other kinds of food.

When it comes to an edible landscape, there are several plants to choose from. Among these are the following: chokeberry, almond, apple, bamboo, cherry, blueberry, currant, chestnut, gooseberry, loquat, lovage, medlar, grape, fig, dandelion, peach, pecan, plum, raisin tree, rose hips, rosemary, sage, strawberry, pineapple guava and pistachio among others.

While the idea of an edible landscape used to be inconceivable, these days it is alive and present in both cool and warm climates. It does not only create an attractive and beautiful landscape but also give you food that these plants bear. You can find endless combinations and unusual fruit trees like persimmon, quince and pawpaw truly enhance even the most stubborn and featureless landscape.

Here are some principles that you should take into consideration when creating an edible landscape:

1. Select a variety of crops with opposing form, foliage, flowers and color.

2. Plant in layers and provide a canopy for climbing plants, middle layer formedium height plants and a ground-hugging layer under.

3. Make room for some architectural plants to provide the display of a truepresence.

You can use several kinds of edible plants to replace different characteristics of conventional landscaping. Use fruit trees instead of standard trees. You can also use perpetual herbs instead of shrubs and ground covers and can be used to replace border, flowers and other accents.

Mix edible plants with other plants to create a beautiful combination. Several edible plants make wonderful additions to your flower garden and create different looks. Today, there are more varieties of wonderful edible plants than before. The newer and rare fruits and vegetables let you pick out plants that are specifically suitable to your garden site and needs.

Planting a landscape can be done in many ways. But the beauty it brings has got something to do with the kind of plants being mixed and match. The use of flowers, trees and shrubs is a typical combination of plants will be organized to create a theme that will bring harmony to all the elements present inside and outside your homes.

Plenty of modern landscaping has caught the attention of many homeowners. But more and more people have created a modern twist on the most basic type of landscaping; that is the use of edible plants.

This type of landscaping tactics has rendered plenty of advantages for any homeowner. It has proven to make homes look great, and it has also succeeded in making your meals more palatable.

If you plan to make this as a project, read through this article and learn more about the plants that you can use. Read on further to get hints on how to maintain them basically.

1. Herbs- Do you want to go organic with your meals and do away withpreserves? Then take this: plant herbs in your backyard and you will have unending days of great food.

What is good about them is that they smell good and they don't need to take up a big portion of your land to be able to grow well. Even if you live in a condominium or apartments, you can have a bundle of them just by putting them in a container.

2. Vegetables- vegetables makes your landscape colorful. Lettuce, eggplants,squash and others can really create a good impact.

3. Fruit trees and shrubs- Do you like the idea of Eden? Do you want a placewhere you can just pick your fruits fresh from your backyard? Well, plant fruit trees or shrubs. The beauty it brings is just outstanding as it is able to bring different dimensions, layers and shades to your backyard.

4. Vines- There are plenty of fruits and vegetables that grow in vines. Squash, strawberries, grapes and passion fruits are a perfect example of these plants. The greatness about vines is its capability to invade naked parts of your outdoors. It envelops them and creates an elegant look; adding more shade and visual appeal as well.

Maintaining your edible plants can be as simple as getting to know the species of your plants, the kind of fertilizer to use and readily available water supply. Take note: some plants may not grow well when frequently hit by direct sunlight. Some may just do well in shady areas. You also need to consider your financial capacity. Creating the most beautiful gardens is an investment. And maintenance surely would involve some cash. Lastly, you need to have a commitment. This is most important if you plan to maintain your edible landscape organically. It would definitely involve great effort in keeping away those nasty weeds and making of organic fertilizers.

The above-mentioned plants are just some that you can use. Pretty sure there are plenty other edible plants that you can mix and match. It is necessary that you test your soil to know if the plants you want to surround your homes can survive the condition. This is a very useful consideration as the impact of your landscaping can only be as good as how healthy your plants are.

Hedges and fences are great for and edible landscape, and you can also use current structures to rain raspberries, gooseberries and currants along the fence. If you do not have a fence, you can plant fruiting and living hedgerow. Rugosas are terrific as resistant blocks. High bush cranberries, blueberries and raspberries continue to be solid as they grow and easy to set up in a garden. Consider the needs and growing habits of each plant.

Edible landscaping does not only add a stimulating variation to gardening but also augments the well-being and health of your family. It would be wonderful and satisfying to be able to pick your food from your very own garden.

Chapter 12: Berries and Weeds for My Edible Landscape

Blueberry, Lowbush (Viburnum Angustifolium)

Blueberries as a ground cover? Absolutely!

Botanical Information: Perennial

This plant is hardy in zones 3–7, although some areas report hardiness to zone 2. It is a self-pollinator that does better with cross-pollination, so for the best fruiting, plant multiple plants.

Growing Guide

Lowbush blueberry makes an attractive, woody ground cover under shrubs or trees, although it doesn't smother weeds as completely as other ground covers. It is the perfect ground cover choice for other acid-loving plants like camellias. It looks great year-round, and it needs very little maintenance. Lowbush tolerates up to part shade, but fruits best in dappled shade to a fuller sun.

Plant already-started lowbush blueberries in the fall or early spring, and amend the soil if needed to create the proper acidity level. If your soil is more alkaline than the 4.5–5.5 pH blueberries prefer, dig a larger-thanneeded hole, and fill in the extra space with a mix of soil made for acidic soil-loving plants. Or create your own with peat moss, pine needles, chopped oak leaves, and so on. These blueberries will spread via underground runners and suckers to fill in the gaps between your starts over the next couple years.

Maintenance is simple. If you want the best fruit production, prune your lowbush blueberries by half each year as the plants bear fruit best on yearold shoots. If you prune all the plants at once, you'll set back your fruit production. Blueberries are very shallow-rooted so the biggest danger would be allowing them to dry out. Use acidic mulch like chopped oak leaves or pine needles to help preserve water. Test and amend the soil once a year as needed to keep the acidity level where it needs to be, and your blueberries will probably be happy campers.

Blueberries have lovely spring flowers, deep green foliage, and lovely fall color. Harvest the berries when they are totally ripe in mid-to-late summer and eat! You will know when they are ripe because they will easily fall into your hand. You'll have to move quickly to beat the birds though. Planting them close by the house can help prevent some of this predation.

Grapes (Vitis spp.)

Grapes need a sturdy support since they are heavy, perennial fruit-bearing vines. Photo courtesy of Alfred Diem.

Botanical Information: Perennial

American or Fox grape (Vitis labrusca) are hardy in zones 3–7.

European grapes (Vitis vinifera) are hardy in zones 7–10, although select varieties have been bred for more cold tolerance.

Muscadine grapes (Vitis rotundifolia) are hardy in zones 7–9.

American hybrids are generally crossing between the V. Labrusca and V. Vinifera in order to increase cold-hardiness of vineyard, fruitful vines. These hybrids typically fall in hardiness zones around 5–10.

Growing Guide

Grapes fruit best in full sun. When grown as companions with fruit trees, they grow all the way to the top of the canopy to reach the sunlight. For this reason, I prefer to grow them along a sunny fence or up a trellis or sturdy arbor. Note that grapes are large vines and will develop heavy thick oldwood trunks, so any support you create for them will need to be study enough to bear the weight.

Fox grapes are North American native growing plants found along the East coast. Concord is a variety that many people will be familiar with and makes excellent jelly or juice. Most grape varieties are self-fruitful, although Muscadines sometimes require pollination from a male plant. Muscadines are also native to North America and were found in the Southwest, so you can see how they are more tolerant of the dry heat found there. We have them wild here in Oklahoma.

Training a grape up an arbor or along a fence takes some care and attention the few first years, but once the plants are well-established, they are easy to maintain and do not require too much pampering. If you plant varieties particularly suited to your growing season you will have a lot more success with fewer headaches. Check with your local county extension office to get some ideas of what works well in your region.

To train your grapes, plant them near your support beams or poles and then train the strongest stem straight up the trellis to become the "trunk" of your grape vine. Allow side shoots to develop at regular intervals where fence beams are, or support beams on an arbor fall, but keep them trimmed to size so they don't grow too wide for the space. Each of these stems becomes a permanent branch across the top of the arbor or beam of the fence and is called a cordon. This process takes two years.

To maximize your fruit production, prune your grapes in late winter each year to keep the side branches trimmed back so fruiting occurs near the cordon and the vine doesn't overwhelm the arbor. Each year new fruit will be carried on the new shoots that grow from the cordon. You'll have lovely shade under your arbor, plus fruit for your table. Expect anywhere from 7– 25 pounds of grapes beginning in year five, depending on the variety you grow.

Kiwi (Actinidia spp.)

Kiwifruit grows on deciduous vines and there are four main varieties that have varying zones of hardiness. You can expect to harvest 50–150 pounds of fruit per plant from these prolific vines except for Super-hardy kiwifruit, which produces about 10 pounds on average. All kiwifruit bear fruit on the female plants but need a male plant nearby to provide pollination.

Kiwi plants are both delicious and edible as well. Photo courtesy of Wendy Cutler.

BOTANICAL INFO: Perennial Deciduous Vine

Kiwifruit (Actinidia deliciosa)- Hardy zones 7-9

Golden kiwifruit (Actinidia chinensis)—Hardy zones 8-10

Hardy kiwifruit (Actinidia arguta)—Hardy zones 4-9

Super-hardy kiwifruit (Actinidia kolomikta)—Hardy zones 3-7

Growing Guide

Plant kiwifruit as bare-root plants in the winter or early spring. They do not tolerate salinity well and want regular watering. Space them 15 feet apart and plant them in full-sun.

Only the variegated leaves of the male plant may want some light shade protection where temperatures get above 100 degrees.

Provide your kiwi vines with a sturdy support that can support them. The vines have strong, twisting stems that will develop woody stems with interesting peeling bark over time. This texture adds to their winter interest in the landscape. Prune old wood out every third or fourth year on a rotating basis so you are never trimming all the old shoots in one season. This will keep the plant in good vigor for many years.

Depending on the growth rate of your kiwifruit vines and your growing zone, you may need to prune the vine tips to inhibit growth. Some growths in the wild reportedly get up to 100 feet to reach the light above the canopies of the trees!

Lingonberry (Vaccinium Vitis-Idaea)

Lingonberries are related to blueberries and make beautiful, evergreen ground cover if you have the right climate.

Botanical Information: Evergreen Perennial

Lingonberry is hardy in zones 4–7 and is a woody, shrubby ground cover that grows only a few inches tall, to 1-foot maximum height. It's an excellent foundation ground cover in full sun to part shade, depending on the strength of your summer heat.

Growing Guide

Provide lingonberry with rich soil full of organic matter that is moist and acidic. It will do beautifully as a ground cover where blueberries and camellias thrive. Elemental sulfur is a good amendment that you can add to the soil to increase the acidity level as needed. Space your plants about 2 feet apart and they will slowly grow and fill in the gaps.

Lingonberries are sensitive to being transplanted, usually due to underwatering in the first year. Keep the ground watered well enough to support the plants until their shallow root system can become better established. Mulch plants well to smother out weeds that will compete them out or take the water they need the first year. These are definitely not the ground covers you want in a drought area.

Healthy leaves are bright, glossy green and make an excellent foil to show off flowering shrubs in your garden. In the spring, the new foliage growth can be red-tinged. Sometimes the fall foliage will turn orange or reddish color. It's underused in the landscape in my opinion. It doesn't do well in my area's blistering triple-digit summers, but if you have cooler summers definitely try this ground cover.

Strawberry (Fragaria spp.)

Long a part of cottage gardens and kitchen gardens, the strawberry plant may seem relatively small, but it produces some of the most popular soft fruit you can grow.

Botanical Information: Short-Lived Perennial

Garden Strawberry (Fragaria ananassa)—Comes in three categories: Dayneutral, spring-bearing, and ever-bearing.

Alpine Strawberry (Fragaria vesca or sometimes Fragaria alpina)

Growing Guide

Strawberries are unsung heroes of the edible landscape. They are beautiful, clumping herbaceous plants that stay small enough to be easily contained, have charming apple-like blooms, and of course, produce delicious fruit.

Plant strawberry crowns or roots in the late fall where winters are mild. In cooler climates, plant in early spring as soon as you can work the soil.

Strawberries tolerate cold weather well but will stop producing flowers and fruit when the weather gets above 90 degrees. Therefore, all varieties, especially Alpines, will appreciate a little bit of evening shade in hotter climates. A good layer of mulch over the garden soil is always appreciated as well. Keep the soil consistently moist and water at ground level to help prevent spreading diseases.

Strawberries don't need nitrogen-rich fertilizers if you want plenty of fruit, but will benefit from growing in soil that is well amended with plenty of organic matter. For spring-bearing and ever-bearing strawberries, you can remove the flowers the first year to allow better root development. You'll end up with more berries the following year. Although I must be honest, I usually forget to do this. I've started planting Alpine berries so I can stop fussing with this type of "pruning" altogether.

I love to use strawberries as border or edging plants. They mix well interplanted between larger perennials and shrubs as a ground cover as well. I've also seen some amazing hanging baskets with strawberries, but in our area, they dry out too quickly to be practical. Day-neutral and Alpines will provide a longer-lasting harvest over several weeks in the spring and summer versus a single flush of berries. The garden berries typically need full sun for best berry production, while Alpines tolerate shade much better.

Alpines are clumping strawberries that do not send out runners, but some strawberries do. If your strawberries send out runners, let the new plants at the end begin to take root, and then cut the runner to create a brand-new plant. Strawberries tend to die out after a few years, so these new plants will keep a bed renewed. Sometimes digging the main strawberry plant and dividing it will help renew waning strawberries.

Chapter 13: Tips and Tricks for Growing Healthy Herbs and Vegetables

"An ounce of prevention equals a pound of cure." This is very true for Hydroponics system, which is a must during the initial setup phase. If from the starting enough attention is emphasized, then the chances of yield grow doubles.

Sometimes, you see that despite having complete hydroponic equipment and care, the overall results are not satisfactory, which is not worth and waste your time and money as well.

The gardening of hydroponic is that type of planting which uses the waterbased medium to grow crops. This method is a soil-less method which is using a solution of water-based nutrient for growing plants like varied fruits and vegetables.

To get the optimum results out of the hydroponic system, you must know the right way of growing hydroponic plants so that they will yield more crops. Many individuals quickly get disappointed with hydroponic gardening, amateur growth, and as they are beginners. However, the reason for this disappointment can be one of these:

1. Lack of ability- for hydroponics system you need experience, or you don'thave sufficient equipment or supplies.

2. Unorganized- you know everything regards to hydroponic gardening, but you want to put forth the maximum effort into it.

3. May be lack of knowledge- means you don't have enough experience concerning hydroponics gardening.

Let's put some light on the varied hydroponic tips and tricks in below points by which you can become an expert and fulfill your dreams: -

1. Choosing the right type of crop

In the technique of the hydroponic system, almost every plant can grow, but as a beginner, you can start with small plants by which you gain knowledge and experience.

The first step is, choose those plants which need less maintenance and nutrients. As a beginner, you can take herbs and vegetables. Therefore, growing small plants can improve your experience as well as learn new things which are best for the future when you produce other plants.

2. Make a proper plan

When you make up your mind to plant a specific type of crop in your hydroponic garden, the next step comes is planning. Means knowing varied kind of nutrients which are essential for plant, various equipment, photoperiod, etc. so that you have a full overview of how it can offer better results.

Make a list of each and every small to the massive thing before planting a crop.

3. Why and when to test and adjust the Ph level in hydroponic plants. Everyplant which you plant in your hydroponic garden only absorbs nutrient solution in the PH if the answer is in between the range of plant which you have planted. However, if the Ph is not up to the mark, then it won't matter how much your nutrient solution is, the plants will definitely suffer from malnutrition and will die after some time. For the beginners, it is recommended that they will check the PH of the plants on a daily basis for the best results.

4. Have proper and sufficient lighting

When you search the market, you will get countless types of grow lights according to your budget. To offer the right kind of lighting to the plants, you have to gain knowledge on that which depends upon the space, the overall distance between the plants, and most crucially the budget.

This is one of the essential tips of hydroponic gardening. If the temperature of the plant exceeds 85 degrees, the overall growth of the plants will stop quickly. If the gardener is using HID lights, then it becomes challenging to control the temperature. For maintaining the accurate temperature, the gardener has to install centrifugal fans, but in some cases, the fans alone cannot solve the problem.

For this, plan hydroponic gardening when the outside temperature is 55 degrees or less. Therefore, it is possible to pull fresh air in the garden. On the other hand, you can install air conditioning.

6. The right type of equipment

First and foremost, one thing which you need to consider before setting up a system of the hydroponic garden is to have proper and unique tools. Likedark area, hydroponic gardening system, an oscillating fan, TDS meter, maybe an air conditioner, a digital timer, etc.

7. Select an appropriate nutrient

You have to gain knowledge with regards to varied nutrients which are crucial for plant growth when you start gardening. Side by side, an individual must know about the quantity of nutrient required by diverse plants or which plant you have grown. However, timely purchase the adequate and right equipment to check the nutrient level of the plants as per the requirement.

8. The health of the roots

The health of the root is essential for the overall growth of the plant. Time to time check the origins of the crop so that plants will not suffer from any damage. While offering nutrients to the plants minimizes the amount of light so that algae and fungus will not damage the roots of the crops.

9. Offering water to the plants

This tip is one of the crucial ones because overwatering the plants will damage the crops. In reality, the water intake of the plants depend upon the type of plants means whether it is small or large.

Crops that grow on dry season need more water than crops which grow in a humid climate. On the other hand, some plants hold moisture for a long time as compared to other plants. So, while planting a crop see whether it needs more water or less so that you can set up the water draining system.

10. Maintain the humidity level

Varied plants have a different level of humidity on which they can survive on their development. So, keep in mind that plants will grow faster and yield higher crops when they are given the proper level of humidity.

11. Airflow and ventilation should be proper

For the healthy growth of crops, airflow is the very vital part which also aids in maintaining the overall temperature of the plants.

Fans and air conditioners should be installed in appropriate areas so that plants will be healthy.

12. Understand Ph first

The understanding of PH level in plants is must get success in hydroponic gardening. Interestingly, there are meters that can take the Ph readings, but on your side, you also have to understand this. The main reason for checking the PH level of plants is that water doesn't have a proper range of Ph by which plants can die or suffer from malnutrition.

13. Make liberal use of your pruning shears

Any time of the day when you see something on the plant just prune it away, it can rot the full plant. The cleaner you keep your plant higher the yield.

14. Think about the taste of the fruits or vegetables. In this regard, whichfruit or vegetable tastes excellent when it is purchased from the market or plucked from the hydroponic garden? The main motive of doing this is there is an end number of crops that don't have a different taste. Either they are purchased from the market or plucked from the garden. Before deciding to choose the crop to plant give priority to those fruits or vegetables that taste better when they are freshly harvested from the garden.

15. Take care of space and type of hydroponic system. Well, it is fascinatingto grow crops such as corns, melons, and squash, etc. but the point is they need ample space. Make sure that you choose the right system and appropriate hydroponic kits. There are countless factors like ventilation, water, etc. are crucial elements which make the hydroponic system successful.

16. Always plant fastest-growing, most natural cultivation, and most crucially which offer high yield in this field, you have learned as much as you can depending upon your capability. This is the only way by which you can decide which is the right crop for your hydroponic system? Find out the seeds which are cheap and yield high so that your profit margin is also high.

17. Explore vitamins B

Many of the beginners in hydroponic gardening ignore the impact of stress on the plants. If you see that your plants are not suffering from any of the diseases then also, they can face stress issues. So, if you think that your plants are facing stress issues offer them vitamin B supplements which are totally safe and with that growth will surge significantly.

Chapter 14: How to Defend Against Plant Parasites

The plants, in general, could be attacked by various adversities: due to the climate or parasites. Even if we give them a lot of care and attention, plants, trees, flowers, flowerbeds can develop problems with the leaves (yellowing), trunk drying, etc.

Often the adverse weather conditions are complicit with the parasites, giving rise to perfect climatic conditions that allow them to proliferate relentlessly. Some of these pests such as aphids and cochineals (very common in greenhouses), for example, proliferate in arid environments or indoors.

It is difficult to estimate the damage that pests can cause to plants, but they are certainly very serious from both an aesthetic and reproductive point of view. These insect invasions have sometimes led to the loss of crops.

Fighting pests means implementing strategies that can eliminate the problem at its root.

Pests, Prevention, And Treatment: Snails

Snails and snails occasionally attack outdoor cultivation and are very rare in indoor cultivation.

Snails and snails are found on leaves and flowers. These animals thrive in damp and dark environments. They are rarely seen during the day because they avoid direct sunlight and go out to feast at night.

Snails range in color from grey to brown and grow to a length of about 5 cm. Their bodies are soft and fleshy, they appear shiny with a light burr that snails secrete to retain moisture and improve movement. They have two small antennae which are the "eyes".

The snails are snails with a shell. Their conformation is identical to that of snails unlike the calcium carbonate shell which protects most of the animal's body. When a snail is threatened, it can be completely retracted into its shell.

These animals feed on the leaves. Holes can be found in the leaves and edges of leaves or pierced flowers accompanied by a silvery, slimy trail. A single snail can attack several plants in one night.

Using micro-pellet products is an excellent solution to protect plants in indoor and outdoor gardens: just sprinkle anti-Snails in the soil, around the stems of the plants or around the pots to protect the plants from any attack. These products are not dangerous for people and pets.

The best way to eliminate snails and snails is iron phosphate, also called "ferrine phosphate". Another great solution is to use micro-pellet snail baits to eliminate the infestation.

Remedies to Eliminate the Green Caterpillar

Discover natural remedies to eradicate all types of caterpillars that attack your plants: green caterpillars, bog wort, cabbage and phytophagous; here is how to eliminate them.

It is a pest typical of traditional crops and - to a much lesser extent - of indoor crops. It is generally green in color, but it is not uncommon to find different colors, such as dark grey, brown, and orange. So, let us see how to deal with it, how to prevent it and how to eliminate the families of green and not green caterpillars that attack our plants.

The green caterpillar is very common in spring and summer and can be found mainly among the plants of outdoor crops, in traditional outdoor gardens, such as decorative plant bushes, and in vegetable gardens. They are much less common in indoor cultivations, those inside grow boxes and grow rooms, where the environment is generally more circumscribed, but above all controlled and clean precisely to avoid the arrival of parasites and dangerous external elements. In particular, green worms attack plants with very green leaves, such as basil, salad and rocket, tomato leaves, chili, and cabbage, but - in reality - these pests often attack rose plants and geraniums. It is no coincidence that, given the spread of these types of plants, they are also commonly called basil caterpillars or rose caterpillars.

Some families of these caterpillars feed on the leaves of the plants; other species prefer the inner part, in the pith, and attack the stem of the plant, in correspondence with the softer and even more easily attackable parts. Generally, the green caterpillars tend to eat mainly at night, whilst during the day they prepare their den by digging deep holes close to the plants which they then attack.

Green caterpillars represent the initial stage of lepidopterans and butterflies. Their body is generally thin (but some have a thicker diameter) and are usually long and soft in texture. Their body is divided into three distinct parts, even at first glance: head, chest, and abdomen. The particularity of caterpillars is their ability to camouflage themselves thanks to the color of their body; in fact, they have the same coloring as the leaves, an aspect that makes them very difficult to spot and, therefore, to fight.

Each family of caterpillars has different sizes and colors and therefore the types of leaves and plants attacked will also be different:

Agrotites:

the adults of the Agrotites are lepidopterans of grey or dark brown color, have a wingspan of a few millimeters, are about 2-3 mm long and the color is usually green, the most common shade, but can also be pink, grey, and black.

Cabbages:

the adult specimens of the cabbages are dark colored lepidopterans and have a wingspan of a few centimeters. The caterpillars in the family of new born cabbages are generally green, slightly mottled and can grow up to a length of 4 centimeters, when they become clearly visible on the plants.

Phytophagous:

You can find different families of phytophagous that transform and become adult Lepidoptera, which take on different colors and sizes. Also, in this case the caterpillars are generally green, but they can also have different shades, especially if they are grey or brown and their body can be up to four centimeters long.

As mentioned above, caterpillars attack the soft leaves and stems and feed on the softer part inside. The branches and leaves attacked by the caterpillar wither because they do not receive water and nutrients properly. If these caterpillars also attack the central stalk, the whole plant will begin a process of progressive deterioration that will lead to the death of the plant. If the green worm infests only one branch, it will die - instead - only that branch.

Remember that plants are also susceptible to infections and mold as a result.

Prevention

How to prevent the arrival and attack of caterpillars on plants? Surely, as mentioned above, starting a cultivation indoors - i.e. an indoor crop - almost eliminates the risk of caterpillars. If - on the contrary - you have decided to start a cultivation outside, the traditional outdoor cultivation, keep the seedbed and the germination mini greenhouses as much as possible inside before transplanting abroad; this is to prevent caterpillars from attacking and destroying the plants at a time when they are still very young and weak. In order to avoid the infestation of green caterpillars - and other pests - it is vital to monitor the growing area continually and clean it from wild grasses and plant residues before planting the plants. Pure Cinnamon extract is an excellent product to prevent caterpillar infestation, regardless of the species it belongs to cabbage, Agrotites and phytophages will be eliminated with the same types of products.

How to Eliminate Caterpillars?

Various methods can be used to eliminate an infestation of caterpillars definitively. If you only have a few plants, the easiest and most direct method to control and eliminate caterpillars is to destroy them physically. If, on the other hand, the infestation is more extensive, and you have already detected damage to the plants (in this case the caterpillars will be at most 25 centimeters away from the damaged plant). The most effective method in such cases is undoubtedly to use an organic product containing a living bacterium: Bacillus Thuringiensis. These bacteria debilitate caterpillars - and other animals harmful to plants - but are harmless to humans and pets. When caterpillars ingest the bacteria, they stop feeding - often paralyzed - and die within a short time. When they die, however, the caterpillars release new generations of bacteria ready to attack other caterpillars. Remember that it is essential to use the bacteria at the first sign of caterpillars.

Conclusion

Landscaping entails everything that is outside the home or building. This includes roads, driveways, parking areas, storage, and outbuildings, fencing, easements, swimming pools, ponds, sidewalks, patios, and so forth. Landscaping is not just planted areas as many folks imagine. It is absolutely everything.

Like our buildings, most landscaping is meant to last a lifetime. Therefore, it is highly important to do some planning. Considering the many options, I am always astounded by how many people show up at the nursery totally unprepared. They say they "just want to look around and get some ideas." Really? Only a truly experienced plant enthusiast can look at a tiny shrub or flowering plant and have any certainty of what the mature plant will look like or how it will perform in their chosen location. When asked for dimensions they say, "It's about," or, "from here to," or, (my personal favorite) they proudly show me a picture on their expensive mobile device like I'm supposed to ascertain the dimensions by looking at that tiny frame on their cell phone or digital camera….Yeah right, Give me a break!!!

Point is, most landscaping decisions are meant to last a lifetime. They should be given the same careful consideration as a new house. Few, if any of us would build a new home without a blueprint. Right? I rest my case.

A good landscape consultant is well worth the extra cost because he or she should be able to save time and money which usually winds up in short supply as projects near completion. Almost without fail we see the landscape budget shrink as time and money run dry during the building phase. While it is true that planting can wait and the landscape contractor is always the last crew on the jobsite, any experienced real estate person can tell you the value of moving into a home with landscaping as opposed to putting up with alternate blowing dust and mud. This is even more crucial at a commercial building site. The more inviting a place looks, the more likely a potential customer is going to stop by to have a look.

This is your home or business and what goes outside and especially in front of your building is a reflection of your personality. If you cannot afford the extra cost of a design professional, you should take the time to educate yourself. Anyone can drive around and observe what others have done. Anyone can find a picture of an appealing landscape and take it to a good local nursery or show it to a landscape contractor. We generally don't charge anything for advice. It is in our best interest to steer you in the right direction.

As a general rule, the more time and detail given the planning stage, the better the results will be. Of course, there will always be the unpredictability of Nature that will be disappointing to some, the delight of others, and most certainly a challenge to us all. Landscaping by trial and error is at best a good learning experience and at worst an expensive and confusing waste of time. Any plan is better than no plan at all.